I0766690

Overcoming Shyness and Social Anxiety

How to Beat Social Phobia, Gain Confidence and Become A Leader

BY

PEREZ DALTON

Copyright © Perez Dalton – All rights reserved.

No part of this publication shall be reproduced, duplicated or transmitted in any way or by any means, digital or otherwise, including photocopying, scanning, uploading, recording and translating or by any information storage or retrieval system, without the written consent of the author.

OTHER BOOKS BY THE SAME AUTHOR

Thank you for purchasing this book. I believe that you will experience the transformation needed with time, patience and consistency. Below are other books I also believe will help you in developing yourself physically and emotionally. There are powerful messages and principles to live by:

1. How to Start Overcoming Fear, Right Now: 44 Powerful Ways of Gaining New Confidence, Developing a Positive Mindset and Reaching Your Dreams

2. How to Transform Your Life in 30 Days: Start Living Differently, Gain Emotional Freedom, and Attract Positive Relationships

3. The 48 Laws of Leadership: Uncovered Strategies Used by Great Leaders to Achieve Success and Long-Term Dominance

4. How to Deal with Angry People Without Strangling Them to Death

5. 45 Killer Actions to Boost Your Self-Confidence: **Ultimate Secrets for Building Self-Esteem and Thriving Socially**

Table of Contents

Introduction 4

Sings You Are A Shy Person........................6

Overcoming Shyness 12

The Good Things About Being Shy 22

What Makes You Bold and Fearless?..........31

How to Be More Confident..........................47

Conclusion 52

Introduction

It takes courage to be brave and confident. It takes courage to successfully express yourself in public and influence the right people. Taking steps towards self-improvement require different levels of courage and brevity. To overcome shyness, you have to be courageous enough to accept change. Never to withdraw at the slightest discomfort, exposing yourself to a new situation on every opportunity.

The emotional change you must go through to overcome shyness requires both physical and mental actions. All actions require planning and the desire to see the good side of every effort made. There will be challenges, anxiety, fear, and even discouragement. Determined to conquer and live a confident life, you must be resilient and stay long enough to prove your fears wrong.

You must be strong enough to reveal your braveness amidst challenges.

Admit you are afraid you are, but do not allow your fears to determine your decision. You won't allow your fears to bring down your self-esteem either. As you move ahead, you will realize the awesomeness of change. You will discover that you have a greater potential when you are not repressed by shyness and social anxiety.

Sings You Are A Shy Person

You can't mix up with other people

You find it hard to open-up to other people. You tend to be closed down when you meet new people. In some cases, you become easily attached to new people when you feel an unusual connection with them.

Attractiveness and feelings don't know your social anxiety. You will meet someone one day and feel like you can tell them anything.

Shy people don't like attention and become absolutely uninterested and nervous in new circumstances.

You dislike the concept of socialism and the conventional acquaintance system. You lean towards a gradual process of getting to know people, even slower than usual.

You tend to pay attention to details

Shy people tend to be smart to some extent. One of the best qualities of smart people is paying attention to details. A shy person also pays attention to details around him more than regular people. The detail is what makes up the environment. The variable factors contribute to create the atmosphere which might be favorable or not to your state of mind.

You notice people and what they do. You notice the dynamics of how things go around and the tendency of it being changed at any moment.

Even though a shy person notices everything, they usually don't get noticed.

You prefer your territory

You don't like to interfere with other people's lives, and you don't want your solitude to be distracted.

You don't hate people but the comfort zone is nice enough, and you choose to be in your zone.

You like being alone, take a lone decision and execute them if possible, alone. The idea of surrounding yourself with people at all time scares and overwhelms you.

In all these, there is a feeling of awesomeness and fulfillment. You don't feel guilty for being like that, and you always plan to be better at avoiding awkward situations.

You love, but silently.

You might be in a relationship but don't feel the need to constantly tell your partner that you love them. The verbal expression of love is not your best suit. You like showing love instead of repeating yourself verbally that you love them. You have the best kind of expression of love because your action proves your intention.

You tend to have a pure feeling toward your partner and do not get into arguments. Even though you find it hard to express your feelings, you like listening to your partner and how they feel about you.

Your friendship is based on comfort

You can't pretend to be comfortable when you are truly not comfortable. You don't pretend to like someone just to be with them. Having a proper conversation with someone solely depends on how comfortable you are.

There is a high tendency of awkwardness the first time you meet someone, but along the way, it becomes easy even as you begin to be comfortable with them around you.

The feeling of uneasiness and discomfort tend to be worse when you meet a cute person, even when you are cute yourself.

You find it impossible to talk to strangers.

Starting a conversation with a stranger is impossible. Even when they start a conversation with you, there appears to be less room for expanded chitchat. Even when you are interested in the topic, you tend to think too much about how the things you say will sound instead of just saying them and enjoying the conversation.

There is a high level of self-consciousness. You don't feel intimidated by the socially outgoing people, but you still want to be perfect when you go outside or at least be like the other person.

You fantasize about being social but get scared to death when exposed to social situations. For this, you always like staying indoors and prefer to surround yourself with people you know when you go outside. There is a strong feeling of discomfort anytime you are in a room full of strangers, even if everyone is a stranger to everyone in the room.

Overcoming Shyness

Make a list

Make a list of things you want to eliminate. Things that make you want to hide your face from people. List your worries about social anxiety and pick them one by one. Dealing with one problem at a time will build you towards social confidence. The plan is to eliminate every single variable that causes worries until complete.

Take the risk

Take a single risk a day and withdraw. In many instances, you will require boldness to thrive as a shy person. Each day, take one bold step that you wouldn't normally take. If it scares you, then you should do it. You don't have to do everything, just take a single step, something you have not done before, then withdraw. The next day, the step you took yesterday wouldn't feel as scary as it was. Whenever you feel overwhelmed, stand still to recapture your posture, then move forward.

Stop the imagination

Sometimes too much thinking causes high and detrimental self-consciousness. Instead of thinking of how awkward you will sound or look, align your thoughts towards what other people also enjoy. You will learn that people don't watch you closely as much as you think. People don't even care about your moves or how you talk inasmuch as you will express yourself.

No one cares as much about your choices of dressing as you think. You will be surprised that people are attracted to uniqueness and they will like you without justifiable reason, just because you are able to break the shell and take a peak of the things outside.

Get rid of the black and white mindset

Just because someone disapprove of your actions or words does not mean the world is against you. Just because you start badly doesn't mean it will end badly.

Unfortunately, sometimes we don't encounter the best experiences at the beginning of the day. You have to be brave enough to seek favorable conditions, and a means of happiness even after the bad moment. Do not push blames either. Instead of leaning towards the negative thoughts, push even harder toward better experiences as the day goes on. Don't make a big deal of negative experiences. Replace the negative with the positive.

Be a good observer

Observe carefully how others do things. Notice the struggle that other people go through just to be bold and look confident. A lot of people who are taking incredible bold steps are not as confident or brilliant as you are. They just learned by experience that the only choice they have is to be very good at expressing themselves and to let others understand them. So, you are not alone in this struggle. Everyone is dealing with one insecurity or the other. Everyone has some element of anxiety, and you can be just as bold, to take a little step to prove yourself.

Avoid negative people

No matter how good you are doing, some people will never stop criticizing you. Do not take those people seriously. Avoid negative people at all cost. Avoid places or circumstances that have to do with a negative individual. Sarcasm can be a very bad thing to your level of confidence, especially when expressed among other people. So, don't give them a chance to make you feel less of who you are.

Some people don't care if they hurt you or not. Some are very intimidated by your success or potential for success. They see a bright light in you, and they will do anything to dim it. Don't give them a single chance. Instead, work on proving that you can be even better. And the only place they can see you is at the top above them.

Be Choosy

Don't go and be seeking people's attention just because you don't have friends. Don't settle for less just because you don't have any. The secret of happiness and social excellence is to have a few close friends whom you can reach out, be with, and tell them anything. All the other people are acquaintances, and you don't need to share anything or do anything with them. You don't need a lot of friends, you just need a few better ones.

Be choosy in relationship

Loneliness can easily result in desperation. A lot of relationships are toxic because the other person doesn't appreciate their partner. If you settle for just any relationship, you may likely end up in a toxic relationship. Once your partner feels like you don't have other options and your whole confidence depends on the relationship, it is easier for them to treat you like garbage in the name of love. Whenever you are about to get into a new relationship, think about your values, your worth, and how important you are.

Put a stop to self-sabotaging

Stop criticizing yourself too much. Society has enough sources of negativities that you are expected to conquer. Don't be against your confidence by criticizing every move or progress you make. Learn to appreciate even the smallest victories. Show yourself some love by rewards such as going out for shopping or having dinner at your favorite restaurant. You don't have to be the best or even better than anyone. The only thing you have to be sure about is that you are doing better today than yesterday.

Stop the name calling

Yes, everyone you know labels you as the shy person. Stop calling yourself shy, or placing yourself where your shyness will achieve comfort. Seek to develop such traits that make you feel better about yourself. Allow the world to notice your genius.

Seek other reasons

There are more than one reasons we do what we do. There are more reasons you are who you are. Do not blame everything to shyness. Being anxious or shy does not label you as an outcast. You may blush quickly when complimented. That does not mean you are shy and terrible when it comes to facial expression. It just means you blush very fast and there is nothing wrong with it. Maybe you want to stay neutral, and you are more comfortable when people don't praise you to your face. Maybe you are just very humble and want to keep a low profile even though you know you are the best.

Don't be negative about it

A lot of people have overcome shyness by admitting it lightly, and even laughing about it. Yes, people that love you and the ones closest to you must talk about your shyness. Allow the conversation to thread on and remain as casual as possible. Feel proud that a set of people are discussing your social issue, and that you must be very important to them. Your progress will definitely affect these people, that is why they have to remain concerned about you. Feel proud.

If they don't know it, they don't have to know

You can accept advice and support from your friends and family members, but you don't have to announce to strangers that you are shy. In fact, everyone feels like you are doing better socially when you meet them for the first time. Challenge yourself to be better when you meet the next person for the first time.

In all these, do not forget to display your uniqueness. If you truly don't enjoy some activities, you don't have to pretend to enjoy them. Focus on the things you enjoy the most, and you will find fulfillment in making friends at that level. When you involve in things you truly love, you will even forget that you have an issue with social anxiety. Because you will meet people who love the same things, have a good conversation, and have the chance to prove how excellent you are. You will have a chance to give other shy people an opportunity to feel appreciated and accepted.

The Good Things About Being Shy

Before you condemn yourself for being socially awkward, consider some of the things that make you a very important person in the society. There are some awesome advantages and benefits of being shy.

High sensitivity

Shy people are very sensitive and appreciate little victories. They have a strong tendency for contentment. Meaning, a shy person does not need to have everything before they can appreciate life. Such trait is very important for emotional and physical fulfillment. You will be well balanced, and you will not make hasty decisions in your career. You are positive about situations that have to do with your progress, even though you find it hard to be like other outgoing colleagues.

Solitary enjoyment

Shy people enjoy being alone. They need to be alone to recharge and concentrate on important tasks. Other outgoing people find it hard to be alone, let alone concentrate for hours with no one talking to them. Shy people, on the other hand, are not interrupted and can achieve more in a little amount of time. They don't have many people on their list to impress by how witty they are. They don't need to keep up to any social standards because they don't need to prove themselves to anyone.

Deep connections

When a person with social anxiety makes friends, the development is slow but deep. They make a deep connection with other people, where sharing becomes easy. This makes their friendships last longer than in the case of outgoing individuals. They value friendship, and apparently people that understand them value their friendship as well.

They don't need small talk to thrive around their friends. All that is needed is the connection, and comfort will be achieved instantly. Even in relationships, they tend to have a better approach to making their partners feel special. They tend to be creative lovers.

Shy people overcome obstacles fast

Shy people are exposed to challenges every day, where the only skill needed is their brainwork. With such experience, shy people tend to be very insightful when it comes to problem-solving. They tend to have better ideas and can get out of a challenging circumstance faster than the other person.

Researches have shown that shy people have a developed ability to cope with difficulties, and such abilities are low to none among extremely outgoing individuals. Shy individuals respond faster and have a pre-installed reaction pattern that keeps them in a safer place in times of trouble.

People trust shy people

Without saying anything, people automatically trust you. Since you don't talk much about yourself, your accomplishments, or the affairs of the other guy, people automatically feel comfortable sharing things with you or even allowing you into a secret that needs to remain a secret. You may be given a very sensitive position in the office, and even your superiors will feel comfortable allowing you to handle sensitive tasks. With such an opportunity, you will develop a leadership skill and ultimately begin to thrive better socially. Since people trust you, everything you say is true, and people will keep quiet any time you talk since you don't talk all the time.

You are a humanitarian

Since every shy person is a great listener, there is always a tendency of high empathic abilities. With empathy comes the ability to understand people, and feel what other people are feeling, therefore treating them well and better. Having an empathic ability makes other people comfortable around you. People will find it easier to talk to you and even share their problems. That way you become a trusted and valuable person in the society.

You calm people down.

Do you know anyone who looks peaceful all the time? These people have an effect **on** chaotic situations, and they make the most irrational and rebellious individuals calm.

Researches have shown that shy people develop such a calming effect on other people. *"Since human behavior is contagious, people tend to appreciate such calmness and try to be the same thing. Everyone is on the search for inner peace and satisfaction in life. People are attracted to anyone or anything that looks like peace. Even when they don't approach you, they will admire you and would want to tap into your peace."*

Note: If you are wearing a mask of peace, consider rational ways to express your feelings. Do not allow yourself to suffer just because you want to have positive effect on people. No one is perfect, just seek for betterment.

You are welcoming

Shy people look more approachable, especially the ones that are beginning to come out of their shells a little bit. People may find you approachable because you don't seem to be a threat to their confidence. Since 3 out of 10 people are shy, you are likely to meet someone who is very shy once every day. You can be a support-system because these people will notice you and may want to strike a conversation with you.

Tip: If you want to be approachable, work on your facial expression and posture. Always smile, and do not fold your arms while having a conversation.

You have the perfect move

Shy people think before they act. So, they have the perfect move and make greater decisions, almost better than the outgoing ones. Although thinking about your next move too much might bring about an unnecessary delay and even stagnancy, thinking before leaping gives you time to make a better decision. You can take advantage of this trait by setting a long-term goal for yourself, with minimum risk and detailed planning. Shyness, in this case, places you in a position of emotional improvement and better decision-making ability.

You are attractive

Shy people are modest, and this is very attractive. You don't show off, and you don't kiss and tell. You have positive traits and unique abilities, but you don't feel the need to share them with everyone you meet. Mostly, people just notice those things, and they become impressed.

Most people try as much as possible to show their best sides but allowing yours to be discovered by waiting patiently makes you more attractive.

This does not mean you don't or shouldn't talk about yourself positively, but you don't have to talk about everything before people appreciate you.

In all these, you have to be realistic about every situation. If you have the chance to show off, show off elegantly.

Praise others instead of praising yourself. This will make you look even better than them. They will become passionate about you without even knowing it.

You don't have to be a doormat. Be assertive and clear about your values. Don't allow people to step on you. Do not allow people to take advantage of your humility.

Acknowledge how great you are becoming. If you achieve something big, realize that it's your expertise and not some luck. Feel great, be happy, celebrate with others.

When complimented, accept it. Smile and be glad that you did great. People congratulate you because you are great. Feel the greatness and let happiness lead the way.

What Makes You Bold and Fearless?

Boldness is not just about the action, but about the mindset. When you are bold and fearless, it means your mind is built to overcome doubts and insecurities. There are evident things you can do that make you feel and look bold. These actions will stimulate the best in you, and it will manifest as a habit, therefore ruling out all self-doubt and nervousness.

Self-love

Love yourself and all that you are. You are not perfect; nobody is perfect. Shift your focus from your flaws and align your concentration on the best you can do to make you happy. Do not criticize yourself. Do not harm your confidence by negative self-talk. Always think more of yourself, and people will think more of you.

When you respect yourself, you will treat yourself better; people will see the value you put upon yourself, and they will treat you with respect. You don't need people. You only need yourself to be at your best, and you will attract the right company.

Family comes. First, friends come second; stuff comes third

Put your family first. Love them and shower them with all the care you have. Protect their interests and never intentionally do anything that will hurt their feelings or goals. Your family should be your priority, then friends.

Give your friends the love you would give to yourself. Make a few close friends and treat others as acquaintances. You don't have to bring everyone close. Have as many connections with people as possible, for the speed of your success will be determined by the number of people you know and their qualities.

Materials possession comes last. Do not put too much value on perishable objects. For stuff comes and go, but only the wise hold on to better things.

It's okay to ask for help

Nobody is an island. Even the confident, brave and courageous ones ask for help. Everyone needs help in one way or the other. That is why the most successful people hire personal assistants to help them in running technical errands. With people's help, there is a guarantee for task facilitation.

You do not have to sweat anymore once family or friends are supporting you. You will be happier, feel loved, and create a deeper connection with these people. The brave and courageous do ask questions. It takes brevity for someone to be vulnerable to learn.

Do more

Do more to people who don't expect much from you. Meet the deadline and even do more. Give someone below you a chance to shine. Help someone in need, there is never a small help. All help lead to strong self-confidence and the feeling of value. Surprise your friend or loved ones once in a while.

Make someone's day by buying small gifts, to let them know you are thinking of them. Be passionate and let yourself go. Don't keep a record of the good things you have done. Be spontaneous about them, and do not expect anything in return.

Appreciate the smaller things

Appreciate the small achievements. Enjoy every single reward you get for working hard. Allow yourself to enjoy minor things like a good smell, a well-cooked vegetable, normal breeze, someone's smile, a glass of chill water, etc.

The best in life come out of the little things we enjoy. You will be happier about your life, and you will stay in proportion. Your level of anxiety will drastically drop because you are not concentrating on the problem anymore. Instead, you are concentrating on the good things, the beautiful, simple things.

Chase your dreams

One of the things that make life meaningful is our dreams. We have lots of dreams and fantasies. Set a realistic goal to achieve your dream. This means taking a simple step each day and enjoying your progress. Dreams don't have to be overwhelming. The journey towards your dreams should be exciting.

You will make mistakes, be prepared to learn from them. You will feel frustrated, remember the feeling; you will remember it when you finally make it. Listen to advice, commit to due diligence, and then apply the best. Prove yourself to yourself, and not to others. Prove that you can be great, that your thoughts can be transpired into reality.

Relax, don't fret

The world is not going anywhere. Social media is full of lies. People are faking happiness everywhere. Even the so-called confident and brave ones have repressed fears. You don't have to follow the trend. You don't have to be in a particular place to feel successful or satisfied. You are not left behind; you are in the right place. Step away from the crowd for a while and reflect on what you want.

Stop looking at others and think of your roots, and your initial purpose in life. Log out of your social media accounts for some hours and do something irrelevant to such influences.

Settle for learning

Since you are not perfect, you must make a mistake. The occurrence of mistake or error is an indication of omittance or missed step. You cannot benefit from a mistake by beating yourself about it or giving up. Mistakes become useful when you learn from them. Take a step back and reflect on each step you took.

Write down some of the reasons you didn't succeed, then set a goal to try again. Your second performance will always be better. Develop a habit of repeating things until you get the accuracy you desire. That way you don't have to be afraid of making mistakes. You will thrive socially, and you will stop avoiding most of the things you avoid today.

Make happiness your choice

Happiness is a choice. If you think you deserve happiness, your endeavors will be predisposed towards the pursuit of satisfaction. Your motivation will shift from frivolous spending or seeking approval from strangers, to making yourself and the people closest to you happy.

If the people you love are happy, then who else do you need to make happy? No one. Once you force yourself to make someone happy, you will lose your joy. Help others, but only when it feels good within you. Do not displease yourself while trying to displease others. Choose the path to happiness, and you will find it.

Be grateful

Confident people practice gratitude. They appreciate every little thing that comes to them. They know how life could be better, and that many people are better than them. They also acknowledge the fact that they are in a better place than most people. So, they are thankful for the people they have around them, and for the things they can afford.

Being grateful means, you are concentrating on your blessings, instead of looking something better outside and complaining about yours. There is always something better than yours. There is always a wife or husband better looking than yours. Freedom is the ability to recognize and appreciate your blessings.

Let love lead

Love is the greatest gift of humanity. People have annoyed you, and you are pissed right now, or maybe you've been angry with a family member for quite a long time. Now is the time to let love lead.

Anger impairs your judgment. Learn to accept people for who they are. Learn to accept yourself for the best you are. The situation is difficult, but do not let love depart from you. Forgive people, even yourself.

Be a helping hand

Forget about your problems for a minute and help someone. One of the ways to improve confidence is dedicating your time to other people. The feeling of importance improves your self-esteem, and you will personally feel more responsible.

You will start making good choices since you know many people will depend on you. It is an ultimate sign of leadership, and you will begin to adapt other leadership skills to make yourself more dependable.

Improve your listening skills

Good listeners are the best conversationalists. They listen to people attentively and understand the meaning of their words and the meaning of their posture. They understand the gesture, and quickly develop empathy.

Good listeners don't argue much. They can disagree with someone, but they tend to listen more to the other side's point of view before commenting. Mostly, people agree with them, because they make points based on understanding how the other person is feeling and why the other person have certain qualities. When it is time to give advice, they never hesitate to hit the nail right on the head, but they are patient enough to wait for the right time.

Allow growth to happen

Growth is the process of improvement in all areas of life. Some people grow while others remain stagnant. Knowledge is the best vitamin in life. There are two types of people in this world, those who growth in 5 years, and those who repeat 1 year 5 times.

Are you in the same position you were today last year? What changed? Did you experience significant growth or improvement? Did you plan or work toward the growth? Where do you see yourself today next year? If you don't have a concrete plan to improve, you will be running around the same cycle.

Let the past be the past

Stop worrying about things that will not come back to you. The past should remain in the past. Consider the potential you have to create a new future. What has happened has happened, and nobody has the power to change the story. Although you have the power to change the future story. It is your effort that will create the change you want.

Do not allow the past to drag you into the mud by thinking about it too much. Let go of people that have been your happiness in the past if they can no longer provide the same feeling. There is a reason they are gone. It is because you need a chance to improve for love and to meet better and wonderful friends.

Learn to speak up

Speaking is not about knowing the facts. It is about sharing your feelings about other facts or opinions. Your opinion is gold. Speak up, and give yourself a chance to change the world. Do not underestimate your point of view. You might be the solution to the lingering problem in your workplace.

If you don't speak up, people will take advantage of you. Be assertive with your feelings, and forward in your action. If someone is trying to irritate you with their opinions, leave the room.

Be a finisher

Learn to finish everything you have started. A peaceful mind is a mind that finishes things, and have no lingering tasks. Fulfill your promises. Make sure you complete your to-do lists before the end of the day.

If you have a weekly to-do list, make sure everything is complete before the week runs out. Leaders are spotted through this lens. People would love to learn from you. So, you will be attracting enthusiastic people wanting to improve their lives in one way or the other.

Change what you don't like

Not everything is out of control. You can be shy and scared and still have control over some things in your life. If you don't want the way things are going, change them. Attain power over your personal life, and you will find it easy to make changes in your relationships and professional life.

Your freedom comes from the responsibility you take of your feelings. Your confidence will come from the conscious ability that you have control over everything.

If you like it, don't change it

If you like who you are, don't allow social influences to push you to change. No matter what you become, people will not be pleased. Be yourself, and the people who love you truly will love the person you are. The only challenge is to become the best of who you can be. Always expose yourself to activities that will bring about improvement.

You cannot change some imperfections or defects. Don't stress yourself trying to change what God intended to be permanent. Your natural defect makes you unique. You will be easily recognizable, and you will stand out in the crowd.

Don't be afraid to apologize

Apologize if you are wrong, even to a kid. Do not hold back your apologies, because brave people admit their mistakes. It shows that you are human and you can be vulnerable and remain strong.

One of the ways to get out of your comfort zone is apologizing. Although there will be a need for courage, you have to take the chance for the sake of improvement. Prove to yourself that you can be wrong and fearless at the same time.

How to Be More Confident

Take action

Stop fantasizing about what you want and set goals to achieve them. If you want something, go for it. You don't need to be confident to be a finisher; all you need is the skillset. Instead of listening to your inner negative thoughts about your ability to finish things, focus on your skills exclusively.

Feel the anxiety and ignore it. Even the bravest people have challenges, and they are not always confident in their actions. But growth means taking scary steps, depending on your knowledge and experience for excellence, not the situation.

Look for motivators

The best confident people have a cheer squad. They are the ultimate support team. Make positive friends and carry them along when you are about to present a new project.

Stay in touch with these people when you don't feel safe. Listening to their voices even on the phone will change your mood, and you will begin to conquer. Among these people should be your mentors—people that will help you in solving technical problems, and brainstorming new ideas.

Associate with people that will support you when pursuing change or anything that will provide improvement. Surround yourself with people that want you to succeed.

Keep a record of your past success

Whenever you feel like you can't do it, think about your past success. Think of the ways people reacted, how it made you feel, and how easy it was to conquer. The feeling will come back, and your confidence level will be modified significantly. Practice this habit to push you forward toward betterment.

Do not hold on to the past glory; use it as a motivation to create another memory of victory. Recall your habit of being a finisher. Recall one thing you did that everyone thought it was impossible. You have proven them wrong in the past, do the same thing today.

Work on your thinking

Stop overthinking about your lack of confidence. Distract persistent negative thoughts with positive actions. Many things we think about are never true and never occur in real life. Your thinking can run wild because there is no physical limitation to thoughts. Choose to ignore every daunting thought. Take action.

Do not allow your belief system to be ruined just because you can't stop thinking about what could go wrong. You have to consciously detach yourself from wrong thoughts and replace them with healthy ones.

Work on your skills

If you don't think you have the full ability to do something, take classes or practice more to improve your skills. Sometimes the best way to boost confidence is to be sure of your skillset. When you have the skills, no negative thought will hold you back.

You can expose yourself to challenges, where no confidence is required. You can practice alone or with people that will motivate you the most. The more you do, the easier it becomes. Be competitive enough to settle for being the best among the rest.

What are your skills?

List your first three skills and focus on them. Take on new challenges according to those skills. Let your ability perception lean towards those skills. Stay safe within those skills before expanding. Once you understand the concept of confidence and leadership within the familiar skills, you will find it easier to expand your horizon.

You can pretend to be confident and fool other people, but pretense may not be good for a long-term perception of self. Live a life that doesn't require self-defense, or lying to cover another life. Be true to your level of confidence, and put value in your comfort zone.

Conclusion

Create specific goals

Since you have listed your ability powerhouse, list the things you would like to do ones you gain a little bit of confidence. List the things you couldn't do because of your anxiety or shyness, and you will get a clear picture of the things you would like to do once you gain confidence.

Create a goal

Create a goal with a deadline. Create a goal to perfect your known skills, and then when to start reaching for new skills. Write your goals down, put them up on the wall. Let your goals be in mind every day. Your growth will begin from the mind to the physical.

Other Books by The Same Author

1. <u>How to Be a Badass and Stop Doubting Yourself:</u> The Ultimate Guide to Greatness, Power and Awesome Life (Self Improvement Plan)

2. <u>How to Be Good At Everything:</u> Develop a Good Memory, Succeed Where Others Fail, And Maximize Your Happiness. Create an Aura of Confidence!

3. <u>How to Start Overcoming Fear, Right Now:</u> 44 Powerful Ways of Gaining New Confidence, Developing a Positive Mindset and Reaching Your Dreams

4. <u>How to Transform Your Life in 30 Days:</u> Start Living Differently, Gain Emotional Freedom, and Attract Positive Relationships

5. <u>How to Overcome Fear of Public Speaking (Glassophobia):</u> Powerful

Techniques for Creating Strong Social
Presence, Staying Above Social Anxiety
and Building Confidence

6. The 48 Laws of Leadership:
Uncovered Strategies Used by Great
Leaders to Achieve Success and Long-
Term Dominance

7. How to Overcome Procrastination and
Get Stuff Done: Stop Laziness and
Perfectionism with These Powerful Life
Strategies (Become Proactive)

8. How to Deal with Angry People
Without Strangling Them to Death

9. 45 Killer Actions to Boost Your Self-
Confidence: Ultimate Secrets for
Building Self-Esteem and Thriving
Socially

10. How to Overcome Worry & Start
Living: Smart Ways to Deal with
Negative Persistent Thoughts, Relieve
Anxiety, Gain Confidence, & Live
Stress-Free Life

www.ingramcontent.com/pod-product-compliance
Lightning Source LLC
Chambersburg PA
CBHW051235250726
48655CB00006B/2779